THE ODICY

THE ODICY

Cyrus Console

OMNIDAWN PUBLISHING

RICHMOND, CALIFORNIA

2011

Book cover and interior design by Cassandra Smith

Cover photo: Volvo diggers move unrefined sugar at the warehouse of the Tate & Lyle refinery in Silvertown, London, United Kingdom, April 14, 2008. Photo by Chris Ratcliffe. Courtesy Bloomberg via Getty Images.

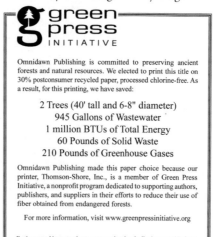

Omnidawn Publishing is committed to preserving ancient forests and natural resources. We elected to print this title on 30% postconsumer recycled paper, processed chlorine-free. As a result, for this printing, we have saved:

2 Trees (40' tall and 6-8" diameter)
945 Gallons of Wastewater
1 million BTUs of Total Energy
60 Pounds of Solid Waste
210 Pounds of Greenhouse Gases

Omnidawn Publishing made this paper choice because our printer, Thomson-Shore, Inc., is a member of Green Press Initiative, a nonprofit program dedicated to supporting authors, publishers, and suppliers in their efforts to reduce their use of fiber obtained from endangered forests.

For more information, visit www.greenpressinitiative.org

Environmental impact estimates were made using the Environmental Defense Paper Calculator. For more information visit: www.edf.org/papercalculator

Library of Congress Catalog-in-Publication Data

Console, Cyrus.
  The odicy / Cyrus Console.
    p. cm.
  Poems.
  ISBN 978-1-890650-52-0 (pbk. : alk. paper)
  I. Title.
  PS3603.O5577O35 2011
  811'.6--dc22

                                        2011026825

Published by Omnidawn Publishing, Richmond, California

www.omnidawn.com   (510) 237-5472   (800) 792-4957

10 9 8 7 6 5 4 3 2 1

ISBN: 978-1-890650-52-0

Acknowledgments

The author gratefully acknowledges *Boston Review, Columbia, Critical Quarterly, Lana Turner: A Journal of Poetry and Opinion, No: A Journal of the Arts, Pax Americana, Seattle Review,* and *Song Cave Editions,* where parts of this book initially appeared.

Table of Contents

This error is a consequence of creation out of nothing, after which the Creator, in the first and second chapters of Genesis, takes all the animals just as if they were things, and without so much as the recommendation to kind treatment which even a dog-seller usually adds when he parts with his dogs, hands them over to man for man to rule, that is to do with them what he likes; subsequently, in the second chapter, the Creator goes on to appoint him the first professor of zoology by commissioning him to give the animals the names they shall thenceforth bear, which is once more only a symbol of their total dependence on him, i.e. their total lack of rights.

It can truly be said: Men are the devils of the earth, and the animals are the tormented souls.[i]

I returned, and saw that the garden
Had not moved from me but that some illness
Of the garden carried it away
From me regardless. I saw its Mountain
Run to dissolution, whose bright garment
Flown from it in shame, whose hillsides lay

Uncovered, sodden. Drawn and beaten irons
Pestering and humbling the soil
Did recreate their brutal education.
All Nevada wept ill-colored water.
From the earth's midsection, giant engines
Dull compacted slugs of gold removed.

Offering no resistance random night
Come at this odd hour, out of nowhere
One by one the lesser cattle took
Their knees amid contaminated forage
Depressed their breathing, and put out their eyes.
I have this against you, Westerners

Gladly, hurriedly, for sums now seeming
Insignificant, (her liability
To second thought a tiny skeleton
My love for the technician clothed in flesh)
The watery component of my blood
I cast from me. Second thought, in fact

Remained and ever would remain my portion.
This is my plasma, I remember asking
And this the money of which the less spoken
I repeated, ending our transaction
Blindingly apparelled, shod by men
Who made walking distances their business.

Repairing to the street, I made me solvent.
Light broke on new men. Sugar giants
Hailed me from the gates of their plantations
And I partook of fruit from their dominion.
Providence became like part of Cranston
Water like a shadow thrown by Heaven

Because the Maker could but ill depict
The foot, his servants he provided shoes
Each according to his rank in service.
For that his genitals wrecked miracles
Aposematic on the vulgar mob
In lingerie and cutlery he schooled them

Lord! they cried, confer unto us freshness
Tone us, for suffering overwhelms us
We contemplate diversionary graven
Markings on our chests and montes pubis
Lasciate ogne speranza, whatever
To break the skin. You are critical

Lord, sneakers furlongs from your shoulders
Behold! that the lesser among ye shall wear the feet
Of the greater on your shoulders: Tracklit
Bending down in aerosol-bombed cloisters
Over beeswax and with Pakistani steel
Shall ye attend their bodies, and in silence

We have no rest. Wakeful is our enemy
Neither solitude. O he is many
No dark chamber. For iniquity
Is always working. Sad irony
We barter enmity for enmity
Alone. Alone we sing close harmony

Walk away, Anthony. Walk away
Alone among the lilies of the valley
Of the shadow of mortality
On water deleterious to memory
Unaffected by renown or money
Loving every person equally

Go now, Tony. Else you got to stay
Tony. Fix a stocking to the chimney
Decorate a tree this holiday
Artificial is the only way to fly
Walking is the best activity
In your sleep is the better way

Bona fide Xtians: please embrace
This poverty of Name, *for* Satan's blandishments
Sweetly shower the ostensible
And sanctimonious, corrupting them
As Fructose *corrupts* their beverages
And the empires of beverages

As Artificial Color *has* envenomed
Their refreshment, Cosmetology
Rendered hostile their native reflections
And the X itself *has* decussated
Images of their God-given bodies
And rated criminal their intimacy

Though that symbol's power, in its arms
And in its legs, has common residence
Together with the powers of Man and Woman
And the Beasts whose going up and down
In the earth, *and* to and fro *in it*
Alone examples innocent traffic

Individuals' behavior shadows forth
Not so much intelligence as species'
The low among them graceful as a god
In the meanest of her done volition
Wordless grammars elegant as music
Phrases barren of descriptive force

Into what could only have seemed darkness
For whosoever had so long beheld it
I heaped my sword with peas. I *put* my sword
Into my mouth, passed vacant sentences
Jesus died today. Or maybe yesterday
The water tasted sweeter in its jars

My favorite year was 1543
That summer I became engaged
To 19 girls before I understood
And with a flourish Nicolai removed
The earth but left us standing there
So many earthen vessels staring upward

Because what other doctor had enough
Skill to diagnose the animal
Solely on the basis of its cries,
Could waltz into the past with a seren-
Ity reserved for things familiar
You might say psychiatry "chose me."

The nights continued to require of me.
Huddled closely, I conserved that resource
"Longwave energy." At night the Earth
Emitted it like darkness visible
Upon the skin. The school emitted it
Long nights I repented at its wall.

To serve a universe so meagerly
Illumined I proposed a global form
Encircled by straight lines, whose center held
All places at all times, whose silence grew
Apparent, as if to impugn my grasp
Of a complicated situation

Weightless as holy text, more difficult
To store, unknown in its particulars
In a general sense more familiar
Broad-beamed, tactful, cool, expressionless
Lightly and in turn striking the tents
The night went on along established lines

At one point she upset a bottlefull
Of Tylenol onto an empty stomach
Said nothing, collapsed a final window
And sat down on the ottoman to wait
Out what appeared to be a test
Of emergency broadcast systems

By that time she was inconsolable.
There was coffee on the console table
If you were interested, magazines
Of rare sophistication. I was listening.
Her poetic diction was impeccable.
She was what you'd call an intellectual

My meter must be breaking, for it calls
This brightness insupportable. Selah.
The greenness of green grass is almost like
A form of speech I almost heard
The intimacy of the air approaches
Frontal nudity and I am almost

I am having a mild religious
Experience: I fear no agony
But comprehend a universal wavelength
In the rippling of sunlit water
I stand stricken by the bodied water
The risen sun treads down the standing wave

With what dread radiance do you embody
Light in August Anthony you shine
More energetic spectra through the darkness
Of your servants' bodies than your servants
Can sustain. *Why is it night already*
Why did our house fall down

Elvis was in a better place.
The style of the dog was naturally beautiful
The habit of travelers in service of God
The cowgirls' under the stars, the students'
Caught as catch could, rushed, anonymous
Ever wakeful, bright, obedient

Lightweight, manually retractable
They spent weeks in this attitude
For a time they were like floating. Drunk
Persons staggered homeward through a gloaming
No home to them despite the many ways
They sought shelter there as if it were

Perhaps I will go. I am tired
Of what sets us apart from animals
When everyone can clearly see a music
Of her own invention in the shelter
Of Petrushki station, slowly sipping
Aftershave all afternoon

Trying to stop the music when it struck him
When it glanced away, embarrassed, wrongly termed
Wronged for stars, immobilized beneath
His baneful repertoire, a gentle rain
Of frogs and minor animals whose voices
Were their names, aflame, belts of debris

Falling piecemeal to London, London
Lit "for days on end," days without end
Endless vowel shift entitled *Water*
Bright water entitled to the valley floor
Birds departing as if suddenly
Made apprehensive of their nakedness

It was the first time he had seen in fiction
Something that was not there.
"The birds have flown away," he observed
"How could they ever have flown away"
How envision a scenario
In which the birds could possibly prove useful

...to value what does not exist
Over and against what does is atheism
In general form. Prefer the world,
You deny God. Six-sided, regular,
Evincing perfect uniformity of difference,
His servants motion to suppress the land.

In all respects save one identical
His servants condescend to touch the ground.
Like a glove, His servants fit the ground.
The nature of the glove is to be left
Behind herself by someone traveling
Under an assumed identity

Under the identity the cold
Induces every servant to assume.
It is difficult to put "help" into words.
Good help show the whites of their eyes.
It is the servant's nature to have sense
Enough already to have called for help

He offered her a cigarette; the end
Holding it gingerly to her skin,
He held it gingerly to her skin
For she had not the use of her hands.
"Let's turn ourselves in."
"Let's turn each other in."

It's your decision. It's a destination
Wedding. There's no longer any point
Pretending you and I are not in motion
Through what we cannot call oblivion
Which will be remedied by morning, certain
As solar chiliads continue shining

"It is as though the physicists have known
Sin." It is the ultimate occasion.
Even the animals after their fashion
Laying in cold stores of local ocean
Water go about their celebration
Some because they have no reason

Sweatered and neurotic fantoccini
Bicker constantly. Acromegalic
Solitary and delusional
Yet enough possessed of his senses
To confabulate a meeker partner
Of proportions like unto his own

A Thracian god, for Thracian purposes
Who kept ten million children calm
From his studio's bad privacy
Here retires offstage to groom himself
Compulsively to ogle poultry, trade
The bearded Grouch small favors for small rock

The Grouch besought that rock to cover him
To conceal from him his vengeful God
While hourly, underground, where it was warm
Young women found fresh trauma to relive
Young men teased medicine into their arms
I have this against you, Easterners

True, there was sugar in plenty for two ordinary men; but these two were little else than children. They early discovered the virtues of hot water judiciously saturated with sugar, and they prodigally swam their flapjacks and soaked their crusts in the rich, white syrup. Then coffee and tea, and especially the dried fruits, made disastrous inroads upon it. The first words they had were over the sugar question. And it is a really serious thing when two men, wholly dependent upon each other for company, begin to quarrel. [ii]

I put on my shoes, my belt, and walked
Boldly up the ramp whereon the man
Stood with the sledge. My brothers, breathing
Softly, balked. Since you would not gladly
For your principles, your principles
Died for you. You would have just *died*

Anthony you would have liked to ask
How they knew that it was going to rain.
Your sainted Anthony would have replied
Same way you do, Governor. How in God's
Good name can you subject them to such treatment
Then. You probably feel the same way I do

Anthony. Strike them with your bright axe
And be done with it. Swine cry aloud
For seven travel mugs of unlit matter
For their mother, for her sadness, could
She see them now, brought low. They never could
Talk no high class

We parted ways. Then we went forth abreast
Fanning out, each one minding the ground
Though there was nothing, least of all that path
Leading toward the *pons asinorum*
And over that required his attention
Since the ground was white, like the *pons*

What is remarkable about this bridge:
We who kept no distance walked abreast;
None from his position of attention
Dared break step, though many stood their ground
While some went on. They called us asinine
Who failed to cross, keeping to the path

There is no ground beneath, for that the path
Abruptly beaten through the breast abridges
And diverts attention. Poor, cudgeled ass
Look you my friend how forking from his breast
Wet paths deploy rude bridgework to the ground
He is an ass. He has our full attention

Jackals oversee the pigeon house
Low-slung foxes try the river ice
Nobody recognizes my potential.
Either castrate him and see if that
Helps or else do something for the summer
Crowds of visitors pointing and laughing

Across the moat. Frau Koma is coming
Not as once, yet good as ever once
Poor sprung oracle shot in the mouth
Whose opinion staid, whose memory
As trail systems beaten by voyeurs
The chief figure of whose eloquence

Sort of tapered off, but with this glance
As if we too could feel the old conversance
Like an empty place. And with this virtue
That it was ever marvelous to crave
Her coiled obedience down the supernal
Staircase or stand her quivering in a wave

Another shitty thing about the eighties
You never knew whether it was a movie
Keeping you awake or just a song.
I'll have a burger and a glass of coke.
Tell me what you meant by "score some weed."
Oh, my God, my wallet, in the cab

Anthony. Was it some way of talking
You used to have, a way of listening
To numbers, waxen deaf to tonal music
Since most by numbers judged tunelessly sung
Expletives anymore nowadays what with the cortex
Starving for air, the crisp autoscopy

Wandering a hospital on lockdown
Eating little, sleeping not at all
And inhabiting a state of ceaseless
Ecstasy for seven weeks, a freedom
Capable of loving back, free
As though at the end of a long tether

I don't know him but that doesn't mean
I can't tell you he's not here. So long
As we might talk about the other world
What matter our despair of moving there.
If brown air take us from our long commute
Draw some brown air through a paper tube

Throw a shadow on the lung, I say
Throw dice against two perpendicular
Fabrics of crushed stone bounding a field
Where white polyhedral instruments
Of chance shock and collide, nonrepeating
Names of the short bones crowding the hand

Not coming to us. And when that April
That download, though the progress bar be green
Of cold rain from a violent race of clouds
Unwittingly let spill over the broadcloth
From the corners of a glowing mouth
Sky brown planet hurtling through time

Outlet engineered for driven men
Driven into sunset from cracked dawn
Capitalizing on the many hours
Twenty-odd hours as the case may be
Given over to their operation
Vestibule communicant with restroom

Housed in economically lit
Shafts cut right and left immediate
As by daylight; numerous glass doors
So many not to let the many in
But being in, to calm the claustrophobe
In each not really trying to get out

But seriously thinking about trying
To get out. It is some obnoxious music
General to that place. True their beliefs
Make them ridiculous but you would not
Dare look one in the eye. This old thing
This vehicle capable of kneeling

The littoral uncertainty in being
Neither continent nor boundary
Unfixed measureless intermittent
Crush of water macerating what
On or near the day we lose the beachhead
Estimated to comprise three parts

Gemlike silicate to one part plastic
So what if the dead arts' practitioners
Saw the scythelike arm of this our spiral
Galaxy in glory since unmade
If they had nothing equal to these sands
Silken, passing pleasant to the touch

Transient. With evident largesse
That blue sub specie aeternitatis
Receded into sometime distances
It had rapidly become. And now this
Troposphere, instinct with fragrances
Surpassing Eden's, reverberates

You of patience left to try look here
Soiled intelligences scalped in leather
Unblocked to deadly noon, on which the hour
As the escapement lost, how they will hear
Listed names enduring as the weather
Paltry dignity contending whether

Yet to stand or to let slip their wonder
Wage congratulation on that teller
Whose lifestyle and return of the creator
Wall the city of their minds with color
Thank heaven, in the words of one reviewer
Six more days and it would all be over

Bridge of sighs, embassy of laughter
Freshmen wailing at a fresh disaster
Dying thunderclap of the transformer
Through the salt-rimmed moonstruck aperture
To darkened chambers where they hold each other
Nightlong tractable surf roars *Caesar*

Murder sorcery theft fornication
Nostalgia, there had been greater contrast
Bruited or shone forth were the paragon
Of luminance the sun, or fire, brass
Of volume, thunder, tumbling water, mere
Voices. Whiteness, wool, teeth or butter

Greenness, that of moss; blackness, night's
Coldness, stone's; torment, scorpions', who
Having stricken men crawled all the length
And breadth of daylight sick with grief, sought closure
Dangling unattended daggers there
Before them in the disappearing air

Of the locking chamber. In disarray
Persons cried aloud, as babies cry
When the plane that carries them descends
Unexpectedly. At 06:02
The angel looks directly at the lens
All the screens of heaven teem with snow

If what moves must move one way through time
So must thunder. Yet do we not hear
Several however rapidly consequent strikes
Together as a chord reverberating
Back into the sky obey no syntax
But that of distance opened on their parting

The air, emptying valences of light?
Oddsmaker, astraphobe, are we not intimate
Charged cousins of shadow clouds pass
Indifferently over the land? Hadn't we better
Contemplate current as absence in flux, ordering
Particles into invisible cordons, massive

Artifact of virtual displacement
Fatherless musical laughter audible
Propagated in shook chain, lethal
Splashes splashing glory on the lawn
Astonished pathways open and collapsed
Sounding the overcast vault of the skull

Then maybe the idea is not flavor
Precisely but a cold sensation
In its place, giving way to warmth
Verging on discomfort, not value
But combo per se, no one's saying
Literature but the fact it's a *coating*

All right, some being of superior
Discernment and restraint at this juncture
Might have intoned, might have said, *Computer*
Play me a new music, strange to the ear
Maybe a lot of things. Oh Jupiter
We knew the name alone of what you were

We found ourselves unable to leave
Comments in the Forest of Arden
But wanted now only to hear the name
Of that pale blue syrup one more time
That such labeling could have forewarned
Anyone was totally amazing

For example, we think that many invariant natural phenomena—stars, fire, faces, complex skyscapes and landscapes, harmonically resonant acoustic phenomena, pure tones and colors, fractally invariant sounds such as wind, rain, and running water—are experienced as beautiful because their invariant properties allow them to function as test patterns to tune our perceptual machinery. The brain, because it "knows" in advance what these cross-generationally invariant signals should be like, can compare the actual input with its innate model of the expected input, and use the difference as a corrective feedback signal. [iii]

Rotor wash, or the downward-flowing
Air by which our helicopters formed
Imprints in the jungle grass beneath
Now stands effectively for Vietnam
Because our understanding of that war
Omitted many things but not the wind
We bowed our heads and fled. In this case we

Refers effectively to other people
A habit we must struggle to forgive.
In 1977 *Carter* pardoned
Nearly all the draft-dodgers. I was
Born in '77. That's why seven
Of all numbers is the lucky one
Why else would *Vietnam* have seven letters

Ranch Hand was the name of operations
Also known as *Trail Dust* and *Hades*
In which diesel fuel and kerosene
Nebulized with certain other compounds
Being then developed to induce
On contact with every broad-leaved plant
Widespread, uncontrolled and lethal growth

Rained softly over seven million
Acres of jungle and plantation
In efforts to deny the *Viet Cong*
Nourishment or places of concealment.
By seven corporations was production
Of these compounds overseen; the bulk
Was carried out by people at *Monsanto*

Roundup, the number-one selling
Agrichemical of all time
Is brought to you by people at *Monsanto*.
NutraSweet's another of *Monsanto's*
Bright ideas like putting caffeine
Or vanillin in the soft drink *Coke*.
We drink *Coca-Cola* long time.

Remarketing is what the language suffered
Agonies and died for, that we might
Inspirit dying products with the word
No barrier between food and drug
Blood and brain, flavors, colors, lines
Of sight, fire, product might withstand
What Godard said. It isn't blood. It's red

Red is a stop or vantage in the brain.
All things red to varying degrees
If this stop be played, reverberate.
No redness stands the tolling of the name
By but rings a sympathetic change.
Outriding any word group arches one
Word, however, disentangled, ur-

Redintegrative, groundless, firmamental
'A cried out "God, God, God!" 3 or 4 times
It matters little how. For if one does
Not deafen or wax wood before that call-note
Belike he never knew the touch of it
Or what you will. Father, stay your hand
What's that rough noise in the oleander

Riddle me your bad orthography
And be morphologized, *Diet Rite*
I paid good money to have words with you
Never mind this lady-with-a-past
Bladder-cancer-in-some-rats business
Or anything like that. Honestly
While *Monsanto*'s sweeteners exceed

Real sugar's sweetness one hundred
And sixtyfold and have no bitter aftertaste
I care more for yours. You were the first
No-calorie soft drink and you meant it
By God, by cyclamate and saccharin
Overwhelming nutriment in vitro
White Grape Pure Zero Golden Peach Pure Zero

Respecting the American *sweet tooth*
As Americans colloquially term it
I refer you to the case of *diet soda.*
Nothing else says *Eucharist* quite like
Black seltzer roiling in a glass
Of ice cubes brighter than the first
Water. Only in *Atlanta* might

Random single-syllable names be
Annihilated by the quarter million
In search of *TaB.* Coke's onomasts did good
Now our tongue is blanching in a Ziploc
Baggie sealed within a Ziploc baggie
Of melted ice. Hold our tongue until
We get to the hospital okay

Rambo was the wrong man to have made
Angry, Sheriff. God made Rambo angry
In his image, Lawyer of the Wood
Named for "the sound of force." When John J. Rambo
Bit into his apple you could hear
Operational Detachment Alpha
Wading through the artificial flood.

Rambo invented colors for the vowels,
Asshole. Rambo bled American
Indian blood; some say Rambo bled O
Negative. Rambo. Universal Donor,
Bedwetter, Horsebreaker, Firestarter, Champion
Of Common Man, Painters' Painter, Grass
Widower, Oracle, Personage, Friend of a Friend

Real men take half measures
A real man takes something like thirty minutes
Inside this doll and turns them into winters.
No one loves a doll with thirty winters
Bunched atop his neck but here as elsewhere
One cannot escape the way the running
Water echoes in the half listening

Rock interlaid with bright green
Algae lining the descent to where
Incarcerated, the subnormal persons
Nonchalantly hand out little mirrors
Between the vertical gray elements
On which the modern sense of composition
Would otherwise entirely depend

Render us a synanthropic world
Assist them to the ground, these gentle creatures
Intending present rupture to proceedings
Now is not the time to talk about
Bears and wolves, how gentle creatures made
Out in the library of everything
Written or how on the other hand

Real bears and wolves were making out
At the time having nothing to offer
In trade beside their bodies part or whole
No I take that back as for the wolf
Breath is so much fog but bears' breath fogs
Over the bright lugs bolting their faces
Which are long, to knotted lengths of rope

Regard the tense shift, Hill 937
And my guide to them: wherefore this color
If signature joined will to deed. And now
Now began the howls of agony
Brothers; the sight, the sound of blood, a place
On First and Main, a little blow, a round
Where everybody knows your name, a word

Regarding the formation of a past
As if by design, a once and future
Indicative of less experience
No color anymore, who conjure love
But know only her name, not what she does
Other than take all day to shade a field
With crossing it. The line is its own place

Really. How many syllables an hour
And how many syllables in fire
In seven, how many syllables. You don't
Need to be a physicist to run
Bawling down the lane in shower shoes
Or recognize a broken safety culture
When you see it crawling with clear flame

Reading King's English in quotation
Ancient, colorless and odorless
It ain't Coca-Cola; it's rice.
Next we were asked to drink an awful tasting
Brown liquid I'm guessing was iodine
Oh Papa-san, they cut away our clothes
Wringing their hands, crying out what news

Resentful product with orange color
Among the falling there is jealousy
Invidious clouds swim naked in the starry
Night. Night, coveting the seven colors
Boards and scuttles each the seven morrows
Overtaking them upon the seven
Waters. Seven also are the sorrows

Richard of York gave battle in vain
Agents, Messrs. Green, Purple, Orange
II alias Super Orange, Dalapon
Nou goth sonne under wod
Blue, Tandex, Diquat, Monuron
Orange, Dinoxol, Diuron, Pink, Trinoxol
White. Much sorwe have I Bromacil

Red is the humblest symbology
As stupid as our blank discontented
Inhalation of organic solvents
Now is the winter of society
Black and red identify as white
On the question whether God has fitted us
With eyes I remain of seven minds

RED
ARANGE
IELLOW
NREEN
BLUE
ONDIGO
WIOLET

for Tom Raworth

This universal, stable type of noise was called 'grass' because that is what it looks like on an oscilloscope. To the ear, it sounds like a smooth hissing without any discernible pitch; today this is familiar to everyone because it is what we hear when a television receiver is tuned to an unused channel. [iv]

Downrange, while I was smoothing out my pistol
Rustling, I heard some animal
Massive, cloaked about in tawny fell
Struggle, ridged horns coiled close against his skull
Knotted, there in the white honeysuckle
Grown unutterably beautiful

Downrange. Tony's cover garment glowed
In the sun but he was messing with it
Like a guilty thing and had been made
Badly, twice on the way to town.
Now one heard no traffic save the water
Passing consistently among the rushes

Downrange. Where this undermined the bank
There was the occasional plashing.
Tony didn't know why we had come
He said. I didn't really know for sure
Either. Then I saw that he was hurt.
We both cried and then I felt better

Anthony and I had quarrelled but
I had not gone home. The goddamn moon
Settled her voluminous down mantle
Down by where we were brought up to take
No pay for doing but as we were raised
Tony said tonight I'd sleep with him

In Providence. Some strain in the position
Of my limbs abating then I woke
The terminal that I might find a match
Rousing it anew so I could see
My lungprint in the smoke or frame my lips
To blow kisses through the ragged keyholes

In my hands. I sighed just watching Tony
Clasp the roughhewn cedar headboard still
Lightly again I touched the terminal
With my free hand to watch his gradients
Disperse. From the sixth unto the ninth
Hour blue light bled over the land

These numbers are for my man Anthony
Whose call sign was The Tramp of Olneyville
Capital of the imagination
Tony's medium and my belonging.
His partner's call sign was I want to say
"Zero." Tony do you know how sorry

I was to hear of Zero, how along
The scripted wall of Providence I can
Almost still see evidence of her
Progress there. Often I had this feeling
We were both involved with Zero though
Perhaps at separate times. It's as I said

A feeling. I won't be the one recounting
Fixedly his nineteenth year or listing
Like a broken record all the people
Doing fine despite their being dead
To him by signs given immutable
Autistic power of signification

While the singing of this early worksong
Was to him Anthony more than the others
Envied that protagonist whose trade
Rather was than valued her ablution
Keep, feed, habiliment and intercourse
With men of quality. For his vocation

Also was the care it purchased. Well
Each little bastard in some measure had
Good intelligence, though it was not
What you would call your dad's intelligence
Though the water and the clay whose curve
The slipping water's suppleness retained

Were to him natural as elements
And from him thus, being as sensible
As proof to proper warmth, to his self touch
No less thrilled than jaded. Show yourself
Name and occupation. Spit it out.
Here is my handle. Here is my spout

Again, Providence is like a net
Cast into the sea. So Anthony
Returning from his search a just result
Many mighty works might leave occult
His algorithm undisclosed. And yet
Is not his mother and his brother Tony

And is not Tony's expletive infixed
All the lost and gnashing teeth between
His the function word that deafs the engine
His the dummy pronoun of the rain?
What blue streak of praise from aniline
Firmament to asymmetric Styx

Is not a marvel Anthony should win
Since his addiction is to dexedrine
And he can hold his breath a long time
While hour by godless hour instinct with boredom
Surrenders him an accidental kingdom
Delivers wisdom of mere assonance

Thus one rhyme word telegraphs the next
Rhyme word, ruining the thing. They made
Game efforts to keep their faces straight.
Tony they gave drink; they brought him out
Among the village sons, disheveled object
Lesson in morality so-called.

Like an animal sometimes he seemed
Full of emotion, other times inert
Wooden, neither sensible to pain
Nor to indignity. Later I wrote
A song cycle describing the ordeal.
Tony was a little boy that lived

In my mouth, among the candy shards
And varicolored solutes of that place,
Of middle height, having delicate
Nonrepresentational features
Like the features of a man who sings
In a language he don't understand

What is it with you Tony you describe
Everything precisely as it was
Even the way you are nodding now
On your hands and knees, sort of touching
Your forehead to the floor. "Another's back
Is one man's element." "Another's heart

Is like a horse's legs." There is no quick
Way to another's heart but through his back.
There were some things missing from my room
When I came in just now your pupils seemed
Vanishingly, as it were, large.
The elephant's innumerable scars

Were all we ever talked about outdoors.
And when I broke my mind I shot myself
Mercifully permanent epistles
On temporary problems. Kind of sad.
And how is your internet ladyfriend, one of us asked
But Tony only shook his head

Wonder with what quickness we made public
Oath forswearing vice or other rough
Trade whereas to own an oath forsworn
Burned the throat, made one party foul
Warming what was tolerably warm
Yet where drafts would shake and sicken him

It left him shaken. Fools held out belief
That we could kill for work or drink for food
Self-administer self-medication
Boiling fallen water in a spoon.
We believed that Tony when he came
Would break the animals, the therapist

Would see herself, this album lie uncovered
By that black artist growing pale on air
Over the interval of many seasons
Viciously spent marring loves and days
Fear of losing which he had not faced
Otherwise, whose touch he had not borne

He amplified our weeping into signal
Stronger than we had thought possible
Mouths and noses weeping thickened water
To lubricate those trembling machines
Our faces. For shame we could not look at him
Though something in his mouth betrayed a smile:

Our weeping. Let weeping turn you on
He said, who practice weeping in a mirror
In each detail let you renew your vows
Swatting undead flies in like gazebos
Whose partial shade is broken in a strangely
Reminiscent fall. Be born again

Baby, let those first bewildered tears
Glaze the airlike veil whose modesty
Pasted to your cheek by comely tears
Again for the first time. You know your vows
Like the back of my hand but go on
Ahead and cry why don't you

But you can't go back to the status quo
Ante, Tony said, dropping his eyes.
When at Covent Garden they induced
Me to brew the ginger beer that was
Three parts oil of vitriol, "to bring
Out the proper sharpness of the lime

'Lime,' we said, although in point of fact
Lemon was used—when at Covent Garden"
He shook his head. "At Covent Garden, when
In my thirtieth year of scanning heaven
As a monosyllable I made
Bold to counterfeit the seven flavors

How I let the black shilling drop
Against the crazy badland of the tongue
And broke step with the real. Not to perceive
The terror realized in wandering
Thus into a sweetness that was mere
Trope, one must have been awake a long time

Outstretched metal won the West but rail
Bypassed that claim as bypassing its own
Shiplike in the night. And though John Henry
Created Western Man John Moses Browning
Made him first among equals. The Johns
Sort of blend together for me now

Barren chambers spinning on a crane
Bondsmen contemplate beneath a market
Confusing to us all, who cast our stitch
In time, which we consider as a fabric
Not unlike chintz. Queues of cattle thread
The gimlet of our eye. Cry, Milkmaid, cry

Like you mean it though we can't imagine
Milk at any price, unmoved by sighs
But by the motion of proverbial seas.
I cannot discover this oceanic
Feeling in myself. It is not easy
Scientifically to deal with being green

Some go feral. Some see prophets running
Through the hail. Some refute the argument
From grief. Some swell with vowels, some with thorns
Ashes, ligatures and ampersands.
Some swear oaths, draw trousers on and stand
To meet the day. Some cup the air. Some stand

Strangely unmoved. Some find no explanation
Sufficient. Some being as good
As dead go lowing and stumbling down
By the banks of some dark mirror to orphan.
Some confuse white meat with medicine.
Some know troubles some have only drowned

Or believed themselves to be drowning.
Some Xtian names some stress positions some
Have known. Some build some human pyramids.
Some feel secure in second language since
Who mock at them in school have other reasons.
Gowned men set fire to cities of white birds

To this we are reduced, and less. We stake
Proverbs at dice. At least the habitat
Joining Denver to Columbus is disturbed
Consistently. It's good to see them back
Silently out of your conscience, some animals.
Parricides stare dumbly at some urinals.

"Among three rooms, two elephants." "Sugar
Is the children's vice." At what point then
Precisely did it dawn on you the band
Had segued into "Immigrant Song"
Where the wardens carry black batons
And one must pick the game out with one's eyes.

"The thief alone knows how the stolen ember
Burns." "The hand is sweeter than the food."
At what point did it dawn on you the person
To whom you bowed was her interpreter.
Tell me if we weren't made to walk the earth
Picking out our eyes we were not made

It is difficult to kill a sheep with dignity in a modern language, to flay and to prepare it for the table, detailing every circumstance of the process.[v]

BRON TO LOSE. This motto bore a man
In livid ink across his fists. His name
It was Anthony drinking from footprints
Townsfolk forbidden to render him aid
Worthless spirits given him in worship
Having little given choice besides

Some very choice incense in the chest
In the garage where sometimes he gave names
Discrete to things continuous like civil
Twilight, which habit he could put aside
When and if he chose. They were the things
Rather that could not but go on calling

Anthony. We begged them not to stop
Calling Anthony who might think colors
Many times more beautiful because
Though we ourselves had pictured larger numbers
Nothing in our minds resembled more
More, more, more. What made this passage

Remarkable is that it was recorded
So hic et ubique it was not music
We enjoyed so much as what we might
Have for ourselves. With such art we remastered
Clandestine valleys where the wiry needle
Tracked his harrowed mate. Then would she strip

Her sleeve and show her scars and say "what strikes
Me as amazing about modern war
Is how we also leave the ground to travel
Winged cabins wakelike linear clouds
Trailing formed of violence on the very
Material sustains them, the material

We breathe. But Anthony I have forgotten
These tales cannot divert you. And the men
Sing *Gobelet de Voyage*. Let's not confuse
Our blankets with the soft delicious warmth
Given us to feel between. Next number
Coming up is called *Ship in the Clouds*

It is hard to imitate the dead
Air associated with my friend
And teacher but to reproduce it costs
Virtually nothing. What the old
Cleft sentences and spirit ditties
Prolonged was widely held to separate

Nothing that was not there from the nothing
Quoted from memory. Whereto Anthony
Codifying spirit who ignored
Advances as if it were quite enough
Having invited them or some brave music
Made speech uncouth except for where in passing

Out from din and firelight it resolved
Hallways, vestibules: "The reveler masters
None but his own step, and through submission
Alone, as their rough burdens beast and pilgrim
Master. What vector, Lord, of ownership
O freight bearing down, borne up

Often to amuse themselves, beneath
The weather, sailors followed in their minds
Lost ordinaries. As dice awe him most
Quitting the hand, those lyrics move to tears
The sojourner just beyond whose recall
They lie, or one who loses, motionless

Dismissive, turning now to face the wall
Prints the moving image leaves behind
His eyes. Likewise low sun at his back
Goes quiet on the forward path of him.
Initially the moving shape of him
It relieves in seven ruddy casts

But in the nineteenth century they plug
The sailor's chest with seven plaster shafts
Hackneyed, but producing in the subject
This sense of a first time, intoxicants.
A watery acrid discharge or weeping
As is said to issue from cut gods

He was a candidate for the slave world
Of drug addiction, looking as he did
Ever for thrills and kicks, stunted, unloved
Expected now that he walked in a man's
Body to walk like a man. Take this
Take it, man, because I got to split

Shake this square world and blast off
It's not a party if you can't get up
In videos you see his men's resolve
Go out from under them like kitestrings
Breaking in the prelude to a storm
Then I heard, or so it seemed to me

A voice come from the mantle. Lay down smoking
Anthony. The voice dropped like a rope
Rock beat paper. Time could wound all health
Red promethazine, pink, orange and yellow
Some saw animals their necks laid out
About them in a circle like the hours

Why not remove your jacket, Anthony
After all these years. Why touch your waist
Time and again as if to reassess
The print of what, provisioned as I am
I must recognize as a revolver.
We have more in common than you like

To admit perhaps. What you forget
Judging by this slowness to commend
Signature to form less recondite
Than the holograph supporting it
Is that the secret is still yours to keep
The question being other than yourself

Who else is keeping it. With that I fear
Our time together has drawn to a close
Let's review the things we talked about
My goal for long-term treatment is to walk
The halls of knowledge and regain my throne
In Norway, Dr. Console. What is yours

Long with neither feeling nor distinction
Through the motions of an education
Though he went, came nonetheless a time
To put this too behind him and set out
Interposing distances with persons
He stood to injure, being so resolved

Continuing neither in one residence
Nor loving faithfully. When he became
A felon wandering he would bestow
Figures like to child and woman, mute
Cattle gifted with wheels, globes escaping
Into thin air that bore them nobly upward

Thus. Quickened by his breath, bent
Beneath his hand, the dumb menagerie
Beheld a landfall, turning cheek and tail
Like coin crossing the damp palm of a well.
What unlettered dread and yawning bookends
Has a five-foot shelf of dirty weekends

Helicopters threshed the East Meadow
Patterning with their lame cadence
The several rills. For it was just spring
Newfallen iridescent water sought
Everywhere for some declivity.
In glorious decline the canopy

Made a figure for all entropy
Wherein "autumn" spoke not of an age
But for all time, the very composition
Of data into sequence being record
And instrument of its undoing. These
The florist let me have them for a song.

The dog made circles of his resting place.
The bird shook loose fists at his soiled estate.
He was my friend, the architect of war.
Whoso would require his monument
Need only look around her. *Be still.*
Those letters. *I know them from a song.*

He saw crowded shades then laundering
Perforated sheets, a pallid clothing
Whose cheerless aspect light assisted nothing
Else whose bright colors marbled long ago
The wide ewer surface, *moving road*
That takes us whither we would like to go

He awoke in woods among whose prospects
Numbered neither travel nor advancement.
The ash went mantled in her namesake, scoring
With nail and potsherd all the lovers' names
Into her low extremity. Shade trees
Puzzled over tasteless darksome fruit

Wave, turn, desolated wight
Those are your friends arrived a dollar late
Standing on the bank as if to spite
A transient whose only source of light
Long embers were, breaking of their weight
Into shadows on the turbid spate

He was trapped in a cycle of employment
Deep in the earth, fearful silhouette
Whose darkness as the jumbled hours
Moved unseen among his cohort, fell
Or seemed to fall singly over the lanterns.
The first man in earshot he meant everything

Tumblers of colorful water, private sectors
Flashlit, streaking masterless through dorms
Known things disintegrating in their hands
Known things faking seizures in the padded
Darkness of their mouths. The sirens wound
Back into the base metal coils

That had occasioned them. The bells choked down
Their tongues and were still. Then someone said
We will return no more. They felt themselves
Swiftly taken up into ulterior
Consciousness, hollow without volume.
Typographers would call this space the air

Endnotes

[i] Arthur Schopenhauer

[ii] Jack London

[iii] Leda Cosmides and John Tooby

[iv] E.T. Jaynes

[v] William Cowper

Cyrus Console is from Topeka, Kansas. He is the author of *Brief Under Water* (Burning Deck, 2008). He lives in Kansas City and teaches at the Kansas City Art Institute.

The Odicy
by Cyrus Console

Cover text set in Utopia Std.
Interior text set in Adobe Jensen Pro.

Book offset printed by Thomson-Shore, Inc., Dexter, Michigan
on Glatfelter Natures Natural 60# archival quality recycled paper
to the Green Press Initiative standard.

Cover art by Chris Ratcliffe. Courtesy Bloomberg via Getty Images.
Volvo diggers move unrefined sugar at the warehouse of the
Tate & Lyle refinery in Silvertown, London, United Kingdom,
April 14, 2008.

Cover and interior design by Cassandra Smith.

Omnidawn Publishing
Richmond, California
2011

Ken Keegan & Rusty Morrison, Co-Publishers & Senior Editors
Cassandra Smith, Poetry Editor & Book Designer
Sara Mumolo, Poetry Editor & Poetry Features Editor
Gillian Hamel, Poetry Editor & Senior Blog Editor
Jared Alford, Facebook Editor
Peter Burghardt, Bookstore Outreach Manager
Juliana Paslay, Bookstore Outreach & Features Writer
Craig Santos Perez, Media Consultant